Toward Peace

in

Indochina

By the same author

The Memoirs of Anthony Eden
Full Circle
Facing the Dictators
The Reckoning

Toward Peace
in
Indochina

Anthony Eden

Earl of Avon

1966

Houghton Mifflin Company Boston

The Riverside Press Cambridge

First Printing   W

Portions of this book have appeared

in *Harper's* Magazine

The best hope of one day renewing conversations with the greatest power in the Far East lies in reviving the spirit of the Geneva Agreements. On condition, however, that China renounces making her power, her grudges, her desires and her revolutionary faith the sole laws for Asia today.

JEAN LACOUTURE AND PHILIPPE DEVILLERS, *La Fin D'une Guerre* Editions du Seuil, Paris, 1960 (Author's translation)

[v]

ACKNOWLEDGMENT

I wish to express my thanks to
Mr. Cornelius Dwyer, Jr.,
for his help in the preparation of this book.

FOREWORD

It is fashionable to date Indochina's recent history, and most of its troubles, from its colonial past. This is too superficial a reckoning and leaves out of the tally some figures which count for more.

Certain parts of the world have been strategically important for long periods of history. Nuclear warfare may modify this, but since, mercifully, we do not yet have to consider it as dominant in every conflict, the old rules still have their significance.

For centuries the so-called Low Countries were critical strategic areas. In this sense Indochina has been a cockpit for contending rulers and races. It still is. The earlier rivalry between Indian and Chinese civilizations counts for less in these days, the Indian being so much the weaker. This, however, does not imply that the several countries into which Indochina is now divided have any natural taste for permanent Chinese rule. The contrary is probably true of the majority of their peoples, even the communists among them, if an alternative to alien rule were available.

By tradition and, I suspect, by inclination if left to themselves, Laos, Cambodia and Vietnam would prefer to be both independent and neutral. Were the concept of such a neutral belt ever realized, it could bring prosperity to these three states and confidence to their neighbors. This was the outcome sought for in the Geneva Agreements of 1954 and, though it did not come about, the purpose was right and as much in the interests of the great powers as in that of the three small states themselves. No great power can now hope to rule all Indochina with the acceptance of its peoples, even if it has the ambition to do so. Moreover, the United States and China are each convinced that security demands that the other shall not attempt the role. Neutrality is not a crime, it is a risk. Indochina could be an example where neutrality could also be the way through to peace.

Suggestions by third parties for the settlement of differences are rarely welcome. Yet it is not easy for the central figures of a dispute to stand back and free their judgment from the daily trammels, whether military or political. Thus, though international conferences may not always reach foreseen ends by foreseen means, they can often be fruitful. It was so when representatives of the great powers met, together with the Asian countries involved in the war in Indochina, at a conference table in

1954. In the end proposals were accepted by the partici-
pants, with reservations of varying force by the United
States and Diem's newly formed government in South
Vietnam. At three o'clock on the twenty-first of July, 1954,
the conference was finally adjourned. It had stopped an
eight-year war and reduced international tension at a point
of instant danger to world peace.

The Geneva Conference fell short, but not by so wide a
margin. This book is an attempt to examine the causes for
these shortcomings, set against the background of recent
events, and to suggest why the way of 1954 is still that
which the world should follow and how we may guard
against earlier mistakes. In so doing I have not tried to
prove that one nation or another was right or wrong in its
past actions. This does not seem to matter, except in so far
as it helps us to weigh their consequences fairly and thus
end hostilities in conditions which can be something more
than a fleeting truce.

AVON

Villa Nova
St. John, Barbados
April, 1966

CONTENTS

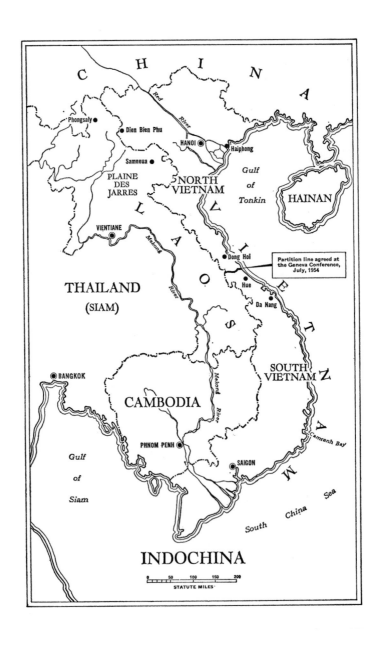

C H I N A

Red River

Phongsaly ●

Dien Bien Phu ●

HANOI ●

Haiphong ●

Samneua ●

PLAINE DES JARRES

NORTH VIETNAM

Gulf of Tonkin

HAINAN

L A O S

VIENTIANE ●

Mekong River

Dong Hoi ●

Partition line agreed at the Geneva Conference, July, 1954

THAILAND (SIAM)

Mekong River

Hue ●

Da Nang ●

BANGKOK ●

SOUTH VIETNAM

Mekong River

CAMBODIA

Camranh Bay

PHNOM PENH ●

Gulf of Siam

SAIGON ●

South China Sea

INDOCHINA

0   50   100   150   200
STATUTE MILES

CHAPTER I

HOW THE SECOND WAR IN INDOCHINA CAME ABOUT

I

IN THE PRESENT situation in Southeast Asia the danger of direct conflict between the United States and China is real. There is, I think, a tendency in the Anglo-Saxon world to underestimate this danger, which will not grow less just because the war in Vietnam makes us familiar with it. The reverse is nearer the truth.

The Chinese have many qualities, among which industry holds a leading place. In negotiation, however, they are never in a hurry and it takes time to fathom their intention. It is not so much that the Chinese conceal it, as that their minds and methods set their thoughts in a different perspective. Nor is it easy to weigh the depth or the sincerity of their convictions, in spite of which one Chinese article of faith is all too genuinely held, the belief that the United States is implacably hostile. To this alleged ambition to destroy the Chinese communist state is attributed every American move of recent years, whether off the China coast or elsewhere in Southeast Asia.

It is not necessary to recapitulate events to show how this

deeply held suspicion has sought and found confirmation. Inspired perhaps by American support of Chiang Kai-shek's resistance to the communist takeover in 1949, it was reinforced by the debate which took place during the 1952 Presidential campaign in the United States. From this it appeared that the Republican leaders and their supporters were at least considering whether they should sanction an invasion of the Chinese mainland by Chiang Kai-shek. Wiser heads might regard such proposals as extravagant; they would be notched up nonetheless in Chinese memories as intentions which they believed all Americans to harbor.

Whatever the cause, the chief Chinese opposition during the 1954 negotiations at Geneva was to any American military presence, however innocuous in itself, within any territories of the three states of Indochina. The activities of the United States, the Chinese argued, were directed against them and not in defense of the territories which the United States was professing to help.

The Chinese response to our attempts at the Conference to agree upon a military mission to train the Royal Laotian army was an example of this stubborn denial of any American good intention. After many weeks of argument Mr. Chou En-lai told me one morning in June that he thought he could persuade the Viet-Minh to withdraw from Laos and Cambodia. China would then recognize the Royal Governments, on condition that there were no American

[4]

bases in the territories. The problem of training the Laotian army remained and, after another spell of several weeks of argument, was finally resolved. It was agreed that the French Government should keep its two military bases in Laos and that these should be exempted from the general withdrawal of foreign troops from the country. There was at no time any hope that even one American military base might be allowed instead.

This outcome may not seem so surprising now, at a time when large American forces are in Vietnam. In 1954, however, France was still the colonial power against whose forces the communists had, until a few weeks before, been fighting a particularly bloody war on a large scale and over a period of years. In this business the Americans had taken no direct military part except through the French, whom they supplied with weapons and sustained with credits. Yet the military presence of the colonial power was to be preferred to that of the Americans, which had to be resisted even to the point of jeopardizing the agreements. I had no doubt then, and have none now, that this attitude was once again evidence of the incurable Chinese conviction that the United States intended a day of reckoning for them in its own time.

Anything which I could and did say, then or later, to the Chinese representatives to deny this false assumption failed to sway their judgment. Theirs was not a suspicion, it was

a faith which was unhappily confirmed by occasional in-
cursions from Washington, or on Washington's instructions, when the Geneva Conference was in a critical phase.
These were difficult to interpret except as impatience or as
reluctance to see the Conference succeed.

General Bedell Smith did everything a man could do and
more to align himself with the French and British representatives at Geneva. Even he had to heed his Government's instructions for the final session. These were that
the United States was not prepared to join the Conference
declaration, but would take note of the agreements, would
refrain from the threat or the use of force to disturb them
and would view any renewal of the aggression in violation
of them as seriously threatening international peace and
security.[1] This ambiguous American attitude caused many
perplexities for the non-communist delegations who wanted
to stay as close to the United States as possible, but could
not renege on their work. One stratagem we had to devise
was to list the governments represented at the Conference
at the opening of the final document in order to camouflage
the American refusal to sign. These and other maneuvers
which were more involved than successful did not, of
course, pass unobserved. They served further to convince
the Chinese that their view of American intentions was the
right one.

The events of the summer of 1954 inevitably aroused

controversy in the United States, as elsewhere. One of the most mordant of the Administration's critics was Senator Lyndon B. Johnson who was, a decade later and in a position of greater authority, to be called upon to face a situation influenced by the decisions of that earlier period. He said: "American foreign policy has never in all its history suffered such a stunning reversal. . . . We stand in clear danger of being left naked and alone in a hostile world." [2]

* * *

Soon after the Geneva Conference, the President of the United States wrote to Ngo Dinh Diem, who had recently become Prime Minister of the southern half of truncated Vietnam, promising his country's support "to assist the Government of Vietnam in developing and maintaining a strong, viable state." [3] This state was to be capable of resisting attempted subversion or aggression through military means. From that time the American commitment to South Vietnam and to Diem became firm, deeply felt and increasingly independent. Mr. Arthur Schlesinger's judgment that the mood in which Washington began the Vietnam adventure was essentially "moralistic" is, I believe, true.[4] Equally justified is his comment that the anti-colonial mood of the Secretary of State required the commitment to be in the main an American one, "lest," writes Mr. Schlesinger, "our effort in South Vietnam be tainted by suspicions of European imperialism." [5]

Later that year the decision was taken by the United States to reduce drastically the payments to France for Indochina and to begin direct financial aid to the Independent States on January 1, 1955. Though this was plausible enough, so sharp a switch had the inevitable consequence of forcing an early reduction in the strength of French forces in Indochina. Henceforth it was only a question of how long a final withdrawal must take.

This was a misfortune, because French influence, under the wise and friendly guidance of General Ely, who had been named High Commissioner and Commander-in-Chief, could have been helpful both to Diem and to the United States. Ely was a convinced and devoted supporter of the Western Alliance, who had served on many missions to Washington and was well known there. His experience and sympathy would have been invaluable in guiding those who were new to the country and in restraining Diem's more extreme policies. He foresaw only too clearly the consequences to which unconditional support of Diem must lead, but while the American Ambassador might heed his advice locally, Washington had charted its course and was in no mood to listen. So Ely came away.

We can be sure that the Chinese watched this change of

overlords and made their own reckoning, which included to their minds evidence that the United States wished to play its own hand in South Vietnam untrammeled by any western associate.

Even so, Diem's efforts, supported by American aid, then mainly economic, did have their period of relative success. The communists recognized it as such and made their plans accordingly; those who once supported Diem so unquestioningly should give him that recognition now.

* * *

In his first two years, until the late autumn of 1956, Diem's rule was bold and effective within certain limits. Fervent patriot and ardent Catholic though he was, austere in his habits and incorruptible, these qualities were not enough, even if they had been repeated in his family which shared power with him. Had Diem been able to broaden his appeal, he might have proved too strong for the Vietcong; but this was not in him, nor imposed upon him.

Two deadly failings should early have been apparent. The army was not trained from the start for the kind of warfare it was most likely to meet, guerrilla fighting. Some valuable years were wasted, with the result that when the Vietcong resumed operations in 1959, the government forces had to devise new methods. The lessons learned by the French the hard way had to be learned the same way all over again. Added to this was a consequence of Diem's arbitrary rule. Officers regarded as politically trustworthy by his brother, Ngo Dinh Nhu, and himself were selected for important military commands and they were not always the best men for the jobs. The United States had chosen some brave and devoted officers to train and go into action with South Vietnamese units. These failures in command were for them often frustrating and sometimes fatal.

Equally grave in its consequences was Diem's inability to understand or promote the welfare of the peasant farmer. There were paper plans and assurances in plenty but no effective action. The scope of Diem's appeal narrowed, his relations with the Buddhists became clouded, and so it continued with deterioration until Diem's fall.

By a coincidence 1956, which was perhaps Diem's best year, was the worst for the communists and those under their rule in North Vietnam. Plagued by food shortages and peasant uprisings against collectivism, it was politically and economically unhappy. Neither prolonged fighting nor American bombing have yet brought the North back to that nadir. This state of affairs may have influenced the relatively modest pressure from communist sources for the elections of 1956, which had been foreshadowed in the Geneva Agreements. There were protests, of course, at any suggestion of delay, but these were hardly vehement, nor championed with any fervent conviction by the sponsoring communist powers, notably Soviet Russia, whose Government is ever chary of even the slightest electoral risk.

Certain dates must now be set down, because, whatever the counter-claim, they have helped to create the present conflict and suffering. "[F]rom 1954 to 1959, the two parts of Viet-Nam lived, uneasily indeed, but at least in comparative peace," said the British Foreign Secretary, Mr. Stewart, at Oxford in June, 1965.[6] This is true, even though the Vietcong was in existence on a limited scale in 1958 and some of its elements had never withdrawn to the North after the Geneva Agreements, preferring, or being instructed, to go underground. It was not until September, 1960, that the Communist party of North Vietnam declared itself by calling for the "liberation of South Vietnam from American imperialism" and not until December that the Vietcong set up a National Liberation Front.

Admittedly, North Vietnam had been supplying equipment and encouraging, and maybe ordering, men to cross the demarcation line and join up with the Vietcong before that date, but the scale had been comparatively small. Curiously enough, this action was made the easier by the Geneva Agreements which provided for an exchange of population, a merciful arrangement which resulted in a considerable flow of families either way. As a consequence, there was by 1959 a sufficient proportion of South Vietnamese living in the North, but sharing the political sentiments of the Vietcong, which could sincerely combine both a communist and a nationalist faith.

Diem's deeds of repression played into communist hands, even though they were exceeded in 1960 by the Vietcong's torture and execution of village leaders, wherever they could contrive it over wide and disparate areas of the country.

These methods, and a well-armed and directed policy of infiltration, soon obscured the immediate influence of American aid and destroyed any present hope of comparison between rising standards of life in the South and rigid ones in the North. Without doubt a determination that this contrast should not appear was a motive for what Mr. Stewart has called the "deliberate decision by the communist north to make an attack on its neighbor." [7] It should be added that the American imperialism against which communist propaganda became so fervent from 1960 onwards consisted at the time of financial aid and weapons and military instruction. Combatant troops were not introduced until 1965, though their numbers then soon multiplied speedily. The first incursion by North Vietnamese combat forces must be dated several years earlier.

The pattern has changed little to this day; the South buttressed by American help but still lacking a positive political message or example, the North fanatic in faith but scarcely allowing life or breath to any other creed or party.

The problem now is whether the terms of any association can be devised which will give security to the area and confidence to the two great powers whose deeper involvement and sharper conflict could be a calamity for mankind. It is my belief that they can.

CHAPTER II

PEKING AND HANOI

II

IN ITS intransigence Hanoi has received thus far the un-deviating support of Peking. There are many western theories as to the true purpose of Chinese policy in Indo-china. One which is specious and popular argues that Peking is well content with things as they are in North and South Vietnam. The United States is now heavily in-volved there by land and air, yet can see no end to its costly military commitment which, so the contention runs, does the American name and fame no good.

Admittedly, Chinese intentions may have been modified since 1954, but not, in my opinion, as drastically as this. If the active hostility of the American purpose is a fixed belief in the Chinese mind, no tar-baby theory could com-pensate for so powerful a concentration of American force so near at hand. It is not that fear determines Chinese policy, on the contrary, probably no nation is more un-afraid, but a natural geographical reaction which we should all share if we happened to harbor Peking's delusion about the United States. It is as if the China lobby of ten or fifteen years ago represented the American people today; the two scarcely speak the same language.

There is still less excuse for the Chinese to regard President Johnson as an eager belligerent. The President has inherited a sack of troubles which he had much rather be without, but he cannot just ditch it. He knows that if he jettisons his responsibilities, the consequences are quite literally incalculable. This has not kept him from repeating, since his Baltimore speech of April, 1965, that the United States Government is prepared to negotiate without conditions.

The American interest would probably accept a neutral belt as fulfilling its needs, but the assurances that it would be observed would have to be as complete as human ingenuity can make them. It may be that from their own angle the Chinese are not so far from the same position. Even when either side can reasonably accept a solution with which the other can be content, a wide gulf of mistrust may still divide the principals. It was, I think, one of the famous Cambon family of ambassadors who declared that mistrust has done more mischief in diplomacy than overconfidence. That is an arguable proposition, but if the international situation is approximately as we have described, it remains highly perilous, but not necessarily insoluble.

So far the President has played patiently and resisted

pressure, which is statesmanship; for while, I believe, China will not seek an enlargement of the war, neither will she flee from it, so that the field of maneuver may not be large.

* * *

Meanwhile the danger is rather that each country, the United States and China, should become fixed and determined in an erroneous conviction of the other's policy. That could bring us to disaster. As an Englishman I know that the Chinese are wrong in supposing that the present Administration in the United States wants to keep American troops in Southeast Asia. Even the immense expenditures at Camranh Bay and elsewhere do not spell permanency in American eyes. They could find their place in the expanding economy of the areas which they are now designed to serve militarily.

I do not feel able to dogmatize about Chinese policy; Mr. Nehru's confidence, which was to be so sadly shaken at the end, and the phobia of the American China lobby, were neither of them convincing to me. The obligation remains to try to promote a settlement which, if it succeeds, can prove to each party that its extreme convictions of the evil intentions of the other are not justified. There is a fair chance that this may be the truth. On balance we can still assume that Peking would be glad to see the last

[19]

American soldier and airman leave Indochina, but on what terms remains to be discussed.

China's conduct on its other frontiers has been checkered and hardly reassuring. Tibet has suffered an act of conquest. Neither its people nor those of India, with their own taste of Chinese aggressiveness, can be expected to interpret or excuse these acts as part of an old imperialism or as a border foray.

The truth is that while there is much that is disturbing about Chinese foreign policy there is also much that is equivocal. A critical question mark hovers over it. We cannot unhappily exclude the hypothesis that China's policy may be grimly expansionist. Our duty is to prepare plans providing international guarantees for the security of a neutral belt and offer the Chinese Government their full part in them. Experience in the working of these guarantees has to be earned; there is no escape from that if we want to limit and halt this war.

* * *

It may be, of course, that the Chinese Government see the contest in Vietnam chiefly as a phase of the "revolutionary war," American aggressive intentions being discounted. If this were so, Peking should have more elasticity in its negotiating position.

If, for instance, the Chinese Government's chief interest

in Indochina is to ensure the security of North Vietnam, a scheme of neutralization for its southern neighbors might have its attractions. Peking would not regard any such arrangement as other than temporary, for it would no doubt count upon the success of propaganda among Buddhist, intellectual and even nationalist elements in South Vietnam as certain to ensure a Vietcong victory in time. Meanwhile, however, a neutralized area in South Vietnam, Laos and Cambodia might be acceptable in the interest of the North. Even if Peking's calculations of ultimate victory in South Vietnam were delayed or proved false, as well they might be, this would not appear so disastrous an event if compensated by a neutral South and the reduction and finally the departure of American troops.

If, on the other hand, communist China's obsession with early victory in this "war of national liberation" proves so strong as to surpass any fear of American forces on its southern flank, or any concern for the limited capacity of the Vietcong, or even of North Vietnam, in the face of growing United States military strength, another consideration has to be weighed. In such conditions, would Hanoi be prepared indefinitely to "fight to the last drop of Vietnamese blood" to prove a communist theory so dear to the Chinese.

For Ho Chi Minh the pursuit of the union of the two Vietnams, which he has faith must be the ultimate outcome of the conflict however long it is postponed, could be of more account than the problematic future of the international communist revolution. For Hanoi and Peking, as for Washington, the solution of a neutralized area in Indochina could have a growing appeal, not as realizing all the hopes of any one of them, but as a compromise which would fairly safeguard their principal security needs in the area. For all interested parties this solution might only be accepted as a staging post, the world would not be the loser if it became a permanent place of rest.

* * *

If Peking is obsessed by its wrongful impression of American intentions, Hanoi's opinion may eventually prove less decided. Moscow's judgment has influence in North Vietnam which can at times balance Peking's. If China's support is the tougher and more resolutely proclaimed, a number of Hanoi's communist leaders are Moscow trained, including Ho Chi Minh himself. Moreover, historic instincts can be strong, however Left the leaders. The Vietnamese might not relish a fate which could relegate them to serve as China's southernmost imperial outpost, even for a time.

There are risks also for North Vietnam in the growing Sino-Soviet bitterness. Recently the Chinese Government have even ignored all anniversaries of friendship with their

Soviet ally, however revered previously. Peking makes the Vietnam campaign a cause of complaint against Russia, while dawdling Soviet supplies on their journey. That is not cozy for Hanoi, which has no wish to quarrel with either communist great power but could find the extreme Chinese demands increasingly prickly to live with.

The parallel which is sometimes drawn between Marshal Tito and Moscow and Ho Chi Minh and Peking is not, however, close. North Vietnam is at war and in no position to quarrel with its chief provider of arms and supplies. Even in less arduous conditions, China would still be the big neighbor, as well as the big brother, and difficult to defy, if such a thing could be even dreamed of. All the same there is more scope for eventual agreement with Hanoi than with Peking, despite the tragic trail of blood and suffering, or maybe because of it.

It is Vietnam, not China, which has had the losses in life and in wealth, from schools to communications. Someday, somehow this has to end. Moreover, even the North has much to gain from forming part of a girdle of neutral states, or at least from seeing such a girdle formed to the south and southwest of its territory. For this to be possible Hanoi must accept two glimpses of reality, though they need never be publicly proclaimed. The first is that the United States cannot be beaten, the second is that while a United States military withdrawal might find its place in a phased timetable within an agreement, there is not a remote chance of even a partial American withdrawal unless North Vietnam plays its part, although a negative one, to make this possible.

Admittedly, the National Liberation Front may have both a loyal following and a momentum of its own. This could make difficulties, whatever the attitude of Peking and Hanoi, but only for a while. Local resources and captured supplies would not be enough to keep the fight going indefinitely. Hanoi's leverage gives it the power to decide.

It could be different if the Vietcong were winning more results, or enjoyed more panache in the communist world. Though brave guerrilla fighters, they are holding their own militarily and nothing more; politically their message is growing musty. Peking scarcely conceals its dissatisfaction on this score, yet, rather surprisingly, seems unable or unwilling to do much about it.

The inelasticity of the Vietcong has been as limiting a factor as the lack of political inspiration among the Government's leaders. The combination of the two, while it reduces the chances of outright victory for either side, does not necessarily add up to another obstacle to a settlement. The closer the warring factions can get to an understanding of what cannot be won, the sooner will modest reason have a chance again.

Peking and Hanoi

* * *

It may be that in spite of, or even because of, the economic dislocation it has caused, the bombing of North Vietnam has created in the inhabitants an illusion of being David against Goliath. This has often been so, in Britain in 1940, in Germany when the Allied attacks grew heavier, more recently in the Yemen, where there was scarcely an antiaircraft gun to crack against the Egyptian bombers. It is certain that the air attacks are regarded by the North Vietnamese with hatred, not merely on account of the casualties but also because, where in the Far East the margin of subsistence is already narrow, destruction which narrows it further is considered the harshest cruelty.

Even so, the North Vietnamese Government would be wise to take a tally of the odds. If it cannot win militarily, it could also lose out politically in South Vietnam if the American hand there is played intelligently.

An Englishman might also tender some advice from his reading of American history. The Civil War was characteristic in the early setbacks, as at Bull Run, and the time taken by the North to limber up. So now effort may be misdirected at first, but once in its stride, the momentum will be hard to check.

Toward Peace in Indochina

* * *

From one point of view Russia might be considered as the country with most to gain by continued fighting in Vietnam. Whatever the immediate exigencies of Soviet foreign policy, the United States is still the leading capitalist power and the citadel of free enterprise. It could therefore be tempting to see that country as deeply enmeshed as possible in Indochina, because it is unfortunately true that, despite vast American resources, preoccupation with Vietnam could weaken Washington's watchfulness in other continents where the stakes are higher.

For the Soviets, however, still more formidable considerations of national interest must prevail. Moscow will do everything in its power to prevent the fighting in Indochina from spreading into a third world war. Should that peril draw nearer, Soviet diplomacy will become correspondingly more active, which could entail a revival of serious cooperation between the two co-chairmen of the Geneva Conference, Russia and Britain. It was so in 1954 and the experience could be repeated. Meanwhile there are dangers in the despatch of modern MIG fighters to North Vietnam. Moscow may think this necessary to assert local influence and eclipse Peking, but the attendant risks will multiply.

The Soviet Government have shown a consistent interest

in the position accorded them as a co-chairman at the Geneva Conference, which is one of the reasons for continuing the arrangements laid down there and offering Soviet diplomacy its chance.

Another motive for using the Conference machinery is that China has never yet won sufficient votes to secure admission to the United Nations. While Peking would presumably welcome membership, no Chinese government, communist or otherwise, would be willing to pay a price for what they regard as a right. In such conditions it would probably be prudent not to attempt to inject the United Nations into negotiations at the present stage.

Let us hope that Moscow is also mindful that the diffusion of the conflict could come suddenly, allowing diplomacy little scope, and that it is a dreadful responsibility to leave the world at the edge of risk if anything can be done to draw it back. Here, however, Russian diplomacy is vexed and impeded by the Sino-Soviet quarrel. Moscow will be infinitely reluctant to take any step which could be pilloried as showing less enthusiasm than Peking for Hanoi's cause at any given moment. Admittedly the role is a difficult one, but it will not get easier and may have to be played lest the worst befall.

What is needed now is some dilution of the conflict, so that we can travel for a while in the opposite direction to the ever more intense fighting of recent years. That will not come about from war weariness alone, though after more than twenty years of hostilities this influence might surely play its part. Two other components are indispensable. The first, a project for a peace settlement which is clear and in sufficiently detailed pattern to carry conviction. The second, a succession of military moves which could be related to this pattern, so that the spring can be unwound, not just as a temporary accident but as part of a prepared scheme of things.

CHAPTER III

GUARANTEES

III

No AGREEMENT can be so drawn as to be proof against every malevolent intention. That is why the observance of international engagements is the first condition of any peaceful society. Once allow treaties to be torn up with impunity and the world is headed for trouble; violators soon have imitators.

All of which underlines the importance of building as well-founded an agreement as we can in Indochina and buttressing it soundly. Three conditions appear indispensable. First, that any arrangement takes account of the will of at least two of the territories and guarantees the neutrality of Laos and Cambodia, offering the same opportunities to South and North Vietnam. This guarantee should be endorsed by the principal powers represented at Geneva in 1954, and preferably by all of them.

Secondly, the Geneva precedents should be followed whenever possible, if only because the communist powers have shown a firm will to have it this way and there is no sufficient reason why they should not be met. On the contrary, some ingredients could be strengthened to give better results. For instance, there is probably advantage in the limited membership of the Geneva Conference. Though the direct interest in the area of some of the powers has grown since 1954, while that of others has waned, the mixture as a whole is much as before, which is all to the good. Moreover, certain of the machinery which the Conference set up, by intent or hazard, can be made to serve to better purpose.

Thirdly, the greatest importance must attach to the supervision of any agreement reached. This was a stumbling block in 1954 and could prove to be so again. My own strong preference would be to keep the membership of the Commission as it is today. The three countries, India, Canada and Poland are admirably balanced politically and have as much chance of reaching a common judgment as any other three powers which could be named to do the job. They have had some years' experience of working together and, despite their limited powers, have enjoyed, here and there, some success. They are familiar with the territories and the work to be done.

On this occasion, however, their powers must be clearly defined and strengthened. The Commission must also have in its terms of reference an obligation to report to the Conference powers, though, in the first instance, this contact had better be made through an accepted and existing channel.

When it was first proposed that the Geneva Conference should appoint two co-chairmen, there was no idea of perpetuating this arrangement beyond the life of that Conference. The Geneva meeting had been called to deal with two wars, Indochina and Korea. Evidently it would only cause confusion to have rotating chairmen to preside over each conference, the membership of which was not the same. Nor would the representative of any one power have been accepted to preside over either conference. Hence the proposal that Mr. Molotov and I should be co-chairmen of both. This working in double harness having proved tolerable to all concerned, it seemed natural to me to propose at the last meeting of the Indochina Conference that the troublesome, but minor, business of who was to deal with the financial costs of the arrangements we had made, should be left to the co-chairmen.

As a result of this accident the co-chairmen continued their joint existence, though there was no statutory authority for them. On balance we should, I think, gain by retaining this arrangement, if the other countries interested are prepared to endorse it. This time, the duties of the chairmen toward the Conference and their relationship to the Commission should be clearly laid down. Both they and the Commission will also need a secretariat.

* * *

None of these arrangements need imply that the United Nations will be excluded from work in the area. On the contrary, the most hopeful development there is taking place under its auspices and needs to be pushed forward with all possible speed. The scheme to use the waters of the Mekong River to bring prosperity to those who live in the region, can be the key to the future of Laos, Cambodia and Vietnam. If once the bold schemes now being blue-printed can be executed, bringing with them a rising standard of living where there has been so much poverty, the minds of men and women may become less attentive to the cries of rival ideologies. This should be a tolerable evolution in countries where, for some of the population at least, neutrality is a natural bent.

Geography dictates that in the first instance the benefits of the Mekong scheme, in support of which President Johnson and the United States Government have shown generosity and imagination, will accrue to Laos, Thailand, Cambodia and South Vietnam. In time, however, they would percolate further afield to North Vietnam. The political significance of this project is that it will set going centripetal forces in the territories which need them most. Economically those areas could then become an attraction because of their unity, instead of a political temptation to conflict because of their division. If so, their neighbors are not likely to be long impervious to such an appeal.

All counsels therefore seem to join in the chorus: press on with the Mekong plans and any others that can raise the standard of life in the area.

The trade of both North and South Vietnam suffered severely when the territory was divided. That was inevitable, the two halves being economically complementary, with the minerals mainly in the North and the food production in the South. The fighting and bombing of recent years have made matters infinitely worse, but a recovering southern economy, joined with neighbors in a Mekong scheme rich in promise, could prove a magnet for the North. It might even result in less intransigence one day, but not just yet. It would be a mistake to try to go too fast.

We have to remember this when we come to consider plans for the eventual unity of North and South Vietnam. These cannot be rushed without the risk, amounting almost to a certainty, of disaster. Too much has happened; there has been a surfeit of agony and upheaval. Time and the soothing balm of economic recovery must be given a chance. A short span of two or three years before elections to determine Vietnam's future would give none of these influences their scope. All would be intent on the imminent political contest, neither governments nor people would have a mind to relax or rebuild. Charges and counter-charges, incidents real or magnified, maneuvering for an early decision would keep leaders and followers taut and on a picket line. This would afford the territories nothing better than a harassed truce, with little gained from years of war and suffering. Political man must be offered some solace, but not at the cost of all hope.

There can be little doubt now that the brief two years allowed by the Geneva Agreements before an election in all Vietnam was altogether too short. Some of us thought so at the time, but the pressure from the North was strong and even the French, with their intimate knowledge of the country, had once been willing to accept eighteen months. We must not make that mistake again or we shall perpetuate conflict while there is still too strong a swell upon the waters. There is no possibility of a short-term neutralization scheme; the same is not necessarily true of a long.

Ten years, or preferably fifteen, should be allowed to pass before South and North Vietnam are asked to decide upon unity or otherwise with each other. As a compensation to the optimists or the impatient, I would add this proviso, that the term can at any time be shortened with the unanimous agreement of the parties, the co-chairmen and the Commission.

However skillfully all this is worked out, it is doubtful that it will be enough. We need to search for a further undertaking, wrapped up in every contrivance of guarantee, to give confidence to those who want it and warning to those who need it. It is arguable how far deep suspicion of each other's intentions has prodded intervention in Vietnam. Whether on this account or to halt ambitious plans of conquest, every means must be used to allay mistrust and to scotch aggression. It is essential that the parties to the agreement guarantee it, but the form of the guarantee is also important. It should be joint and several and, in order to create the most effective deterrent value, the guarantors must have the right in certain conditions to act without waiting for unanimity, should the terms of the agreement be violated.

The result would be a system of the Locarno type and, in order to bring it into being in Southeast Asia, a number of difficulties would have to be resolved, but the effort would be worthwhile. For the United States such an arrangement would involve joining in a guarantee to which communist China was itself a party. It would also mean for both countries the choice of some organization before whom any alleged breach could be argued. The Security Council of the United Nations is an evident possibility in this connection, but it could be that some body of more local character, though including the great powers, perhaps with a membership comparable to that of the Geneva Conference of 1954, or the later conference on Laos in 1962, would be found more suitable.

As an additional safeguard, the guaranteed countries could be denied the purchase of arms from any of the guarantor powers. This prohibition could be supervised by the Commission.

What is indispensable is that we should use our ingenuity to persuade the world and these small countries of our joint determination to give them a neutral character and to safeguard this condition.

The difficulties speak for themselves only too easily but, if once a system of this kind were established, it might gain authority and momentum, until all found it more advantageous to cling to its benefits than to try to overset it, with all the attendant dangers.

CHAPTER IV

STRATAGEMS

IV

IN THE CONDITIONS of fighting which prevail in Vietnam it would scarcely be practicable to attempt a ceasefire without preliminaries. A conference would first have to give instructions to the military commanders to enable them to disentangle their forces and concentrate them in the appointed areas.

The most intricate of all questions in fighting of this guerrilla character has now to be considered, whether there is any military action which it is possible and prudent for the American authorities to take which would at the same time effectively reduce tension in the area. This problem is further complicated by the limits imposed through the restriction of South Vietnamese and American authority mainly to the towns, whereas the Vietcong controls most of the countryside by day or by night. Obviously the United States and the South Vietnamese should not be asked to take risks which would imperil all they have fought for. Some moves may, however, be feasible, even though they have to be made cautiously and their development is dependent upon acquiescence, if not reciprocity, on the other side.

Bombing is an evident example. The bombing of North Vietnam, with the limitations * which the United States has rightly felt compelled to impose, has always been of debatable value. Its influence on the actual fighting is probably more remote than its protagonists will admit. This reservation also applies to attempts to disrupt Vietcong supply lines in South Vietnam and in Laos by air action, or even to bombing attacks by day on road blocks set up by the Vietcong. However complete the devastation, the effect is temporary and therefore not decisive. The belief that one air strike could succeed in fouling the enemy's communications before Dien Bien Phu never seemed to me credible in 1954. I suspect that in the conditions of the present fighting in Vietnam, the claims for the military, as apart from the horror, influence of bombing are also exaggerated. Still less can heavier bombing redress a political decline. At most it could encourage the recalcitrant to the council table, but there is so far little evidence of this.

However that may be, the bombing strategy could be moderated by stages to make such a reduced program tell in the minds of the enemy. Its effect would be the more com-

* I refer to the limitations in force in March, 1966.

pelling if the successive steps were linked to parallel or
related moves by the ground forces.

Here much must depend upon the course of hostilities
and the political progress which the United States and the
South Vietnamese authorities, whether local or national,
can realize in the next few months. We know that the
United States has no wish to appear as a colonial power in
Vietnam nor to assume a parental role, even for a spell.
In spite of this reluctance, some responsibility to guide and
guard cannot be avoided and was, indeed, accepted by Vice-
President Humphrey's mission to South Vietnam after
President Johnson's Hawaii conference in February, 1966.

* * *

Whatever new efforts are made, they need not imply
that the United States must devote itself to setting up a
democratic state in South Vietnam. We should like it
much better that way, but we know the obstacles. It remains true that a freely elected parliamentary democracy
is the only effective safeguard to protect the liberty of the
individual. While firmly convinced of this, we have unhappily to accept that many in these days still pay lip
service to such a form of government, but few have the
will or experience to practice it. It is altogether too testing
a business.

It would, therefore, be unjust and unreasonable to complain that the United States has not been able to nurture a democratic system, as we understand it, in South Vietnam. An unjaundiced view of Africa and Asia is sufficient reply to such a demand. It is, however, indispensable that an administration which has sufficient support nationally and locally to command a positive following should come into being in South Vietnam. There is no doubt of the deep hatred for communist rule sincerely felt by many South Vietnamese, often as a result of personal experience. Yet it will never be easy to enlist this hostility, which can be due to a variety of causes, except by leadership which has a national appeal.

This is the inescapable political problem for the Americans and their allies, and no doubt the Americans know it. As for the South Vietnamese, their endurance has been heroic and they deserve a solution which will at last bring peace to their mauled countryside. Even so, South Vietnam can hardly now be left to sort out its discordant elements in a territory where no one of them has sufficient authority or following to prevail. Some encouragement by the United States is essential, that country having gone so far.

While a more widely based political authority is constantly being sought in the South, this result would be encouraged if all military action in the country were, as far as possible, coordinated to serve the main political purpose, the promotion of unity. This will entail the patient protection of an increasing number of selected country areas and the encouragement of local administration and leadership within them. It will be no easy task where the Vietcong can move so effectively by night, but it has to be done, for no solution is possible based on the effective guardianship of towns alone. However long it takes, methodically settled conditions must be brought, stage by stage, to selected parts of the countryside. They must be given the chance to live and breathe; nothing can be accomplished without this. For the people it is not a question of being for or against the Vietcong; it is survival. It was so in Malaya and no doubt the same rules apply in the more difficult conditions of Vietnam.

When regions of assured security have been established by day and night, a further step in evolution will be in sight. Certain definable areas of the country should then enjoy conditions which are sufficiently stable for a local withdrawal of American forces to be practicable without undue risk; South Vietnamese forces could remain. If we travel this far successfully, we might be at the turning point.

Such a withdrawal could be announced as well as made. Supposing these events produced no unfavorable reaction, the way would be open to repeat the tactics in another part of the country. It might then be that the confidence gained by the South Vietnamese, and their solid survival over a period of time, would make it safe for the United States Government to order a first withdrawal of one of their units from Vietnam. This would be retreat by trial and success.

Admittedly, the outcome could be very different. The Vietcong might, if it were militarily in their scope to do so, seize the occasion to launch an attack on the chosen area. If this succeeded, the American trial experiment would have been an apparent failure. If, however, the attempt were foiled, the Vietcong would suffer grievously in reputation as well as in fact. In either event such tactics would be hard to reconcile with Vietcong claims that all that was wanted was the withdrawal of the Americans, when hostilities would cease and every problem be re-solved. On balance, therefore, this method, or an adapta-tion of it, seems worth following. It is important to take political ground from the Vietcong; the conditions for a settlement will not be lined up by military means alone.

The odds are evidently against the success of such a scheme as this, but not overwhelmingly so. I have seen other situations which at some time have looked equally bleak but which later yielded to a solution. This is the reason why it is important to show by practice that every obligation to which the free world is pledged is kept, what-

ever the behavior of the Vietcong. Prominent among these
is the Geneva Prisoners of War Convention.

* * *

Mankind has made progress in science in this century,
in mercy it has moved backwards. Torture was little prac-
ticed and much frowned upon among nations which still
called themselves civilized a hundred years ago. This ad-
jective may seem arrogant to modern ears, but I do not
think that it was. Torture is debasing and sadistic and it
is a sorrowful mark of the times in which we live that it
should be tolerated in war and so constantly publicized in
peace. It was to establish a code of conduct for the humane
treatment of prisoners of war that the Geneva Convention
was accepted; it has to be respected if a claim to uphold the
rule of law is to have any meaning.

There is also a military side to this question. Those of
us who have served with combat troops know that if anything is likely to stiffen a man's determination to soldier
on to the end, it is the knowledge that he will be tortured
if he is captured. The western purpose in Vietnam is to
get the enemy to the conference table. Everything that can
be done to convince the civilian population that they will
be well cared for if they transfer allegiance, and the fighting man that the rules of war will protect him if he sur-
renders, will bring us nearer that day.

[47]

It is, however, only the known practice, not the promise of these benefits, that will weigh in the scales. Generous treatment of prisoners can tell quite heavily as it did in Malaya and the Philippines, and should be the rule, whatever the Oriental opinion of torture. What we want to establish are conditions in which bitterness can be mollified and hatred assuaged.

Admittedly, these suggestions cannot determine the conflict in so far as it is one between the free world and the communist world. The most they can do is to help provide a compromise, an accommodation with which both sides can learn to live. There have been many such in history. Then perhaps these territories can cease to be "a point of instant danger to world peace," as I had hoped when the Geneva Conference closed in the summer of 1954. Whether we can do better this time depends not merely on the ingenuity of our plans, but also on whether the principals have a mind to give them a chance to work.

TWO NATURAL NEUTRALS

V

The Laotians

THERE IS surely a moral in the recent history of Laos. A sparse population inhabits a lonely, mountainous country and asks only that the world should pass it by. It is possible to mock the Laotians because they differ so much from the warlike hill tribes of tradition, the Scottish Highlanders of the eighteenth century or the Pathans of a later date; it is also possible to respect them.

I first felt sympathy for these people at the 1954 Geneva Conference, because they differed from all others in their approach to their problems. They appeared to harbor neither resentment nor suspicion against their neighbors, nor even to take much interest in them. Stranger still, they seemed quite free of any ideological fervor, neither to want to be communists, nor to wish to annihilate them.

I admit, however, that I did not meet the Pathet Lao, for after a struggle we prevailed in our refusal to accept their credentials for the conference table. They may have been entirely different in temper. These Pathet Lao were communist guerrillas operating mainly in Phongsaly and Samneua, the two northern provinces of the country.

Among those Laotians I did meet, patience and a general reluctance to slit a neighbor's throat seemed to be national traits. Certainly there is little of the crusader in them, which may be why such a sad mess was made of their policies by obstinate foreigners in the late fifties.

The Geneva Conference served Laos better than it could Vietnam. After much argument, Laos emerged with a neutral government and, on balance, a weakened Pathet Lao. Chou En-lai having accepted that France should have the right to keep her two military missions on Laotian soil, the Laotian Government were well content. No doubt they felt that the French would respect and support their neutral purpose. In this they were right, for the governments of France now adhered continuously to this policy through all vicissitudes. When in 1961 President Kennedy discussed Laos with General de Gaulle in Paris, it can have been no surprise that the General strongly supported the idea of a neutral coalition under Souvanna Phouma.

The interval, however, had been troubled, not least because French opinions on Southeast Asia had been much at a discount in Washington following the Geneva Conference. After prolonged and rather leisurely maneuvers, Prince Souvanna Phouma, as the head of the Royal Laotian

Government, had contrived to come to terms with his half-brother Prince Souphanouvong at the head of the Pathet Lao. These terms were embodied in the Vientiane Agreements of November, 1957, which provided for a neutral country under a coalition government.

The United States Government, which had hoped to see a more pro-western administration set up than that for which Prince Souvanna Phouma had openly declared, did not like this shift of events. Large sums of money had been spent, or were contemplated, to build up and equip the Royal Laotian army, some of this, it would seem, at the instant urging of the State Department and against the wiser counsel of the Department of Defense. American aid was denied to Souvanna Phouma, whose government fell in the summer of 1958. His successors, though further to the right, were also more unfortunate. Despite American training and equipment, the Royal army was in no shape to take on the Pathet Lao at the Plaine des Jarres in the following May. The fighting was desultory rather than sharp, but it went badly for the government forces over the next two years.

A prudent attempt by Mr. Winthrop Brown, when newly appointed as American Ambassador, to bring neutralists and anti-communists together under Souvanna Phouma, accepting as a consequence a neutralist government again, was not supported in Washington, though both the French and British governments favored it. The delay and the mission of Mr. Graham Parsons to persuade Souvanna Phouma to abandon his policies were hardly propitious and achieved nothing. Not even a victory for a Washington-sponsored leader of the right, Phoumi Nosavan, based no doubt on sound American military advice, could redress the balance. By the end of 1960, Souvanna had fled to Cambodia, but was still recognized by Moscow and Peking, while the Pathet Lao were stronger than ever and reinforced by the defection of a local commander with his American equipment.

Two more years of negotiation followed, until the Geneva Neutralization Agreement was signed in the summer of 1962. Meanwhile both Soviet and Chinese influence in Laos had increased significantly and a Soviet mission was installed in the capital.

More recent events have told against the communists. Continuing efforts by the Vietcong to keep open their supply routes to their supporters in South Vietnam have resulted in hostilities and consequent suffering and loss to the local Laotian population. This has had its reaction in Vientiane where, for the present at least, the Vietcong and their allies the Pathet Lao are not loved. The final outcome in Laos will no doubt be deeply marked by the turn of events in Vietnam. Even so, the Laotians ask only to be let alone and, short of conquest, however Left their own government, they would not willingly accept Vietcong rule. They are entitled to this much surcease.

* * *

The moral of these checkered events would seem to be:

1) That a country situated as is Laos geographically, with its two and a half millions of population living in a territory half the size of France, with indifferent communications and no direct access to the sea, is well adapted to neutrality between two great power complexes. If, in these special conditions, neutrality suits Laos, it should suit the great powers also.

2) If a people's temper is instinctively neutral, as was, and is, that of the Laotians, it is wise to try to match the policies of the western world to it. Nor can it be right to use economic aid to try to compel a community in such conditions to distort its policy. Where a nation offers no threat to the security of others, it should be safe from any form of coercion.

3) Laos had over the years enjoyed better relations with the colonial power than any other part of Indochina. In the light of this, and of the Chinese acceptance of two French bases on Laotian soil, it would have been

prudent for the United States Government to have
sought and kept close relations with France in all
Laotian affairs. Unfortunately the opposite was the
practice. "Nowhere else, perhaps," writes General Ely
sadly, "did France and Great Britain find themselves
in such constant opposition to the United States about
the policy to be pursued." [8] General Ely's next comment is no less apposite: that the military and diplo-
matic representatives of the United States in Laos did
not always see eye to eye.

There are occasions in diplomacy when to reach for the
better is to lose the good.

The Cambodians

Cambodia, the smallest of the states in Indochina, proved
the toughest in negotiation at Geneva; it suspected all and
yielded nothing. It is true that Viet-Minh penetration into
that country had been the slightest and received scarcely
more than token support from the Soviet or Chinese
spokesmen. The speed and completeness of the renuncia-
tion and withdrawal were nonetheless a triumph for the
Cambodian representatives.

Two Natural Neutrals

The evening of July 20 to 21, 1954, is still vivid in my mind. The many phases of this intricate Geneva negotiation being almost all in order, Molotov and I, as co-chairmen of the Conference, came at last to the question of Cambodia, only to meet mistrust and stubborn negatives. Even the Three Power Commission was viewed with skepticism, nor could General Bedell Smith's assurances, though generously given, prevail entirely.

It may have been exhaustion or a genuine fear that, if we did not finish during that night, all our work would be thrown back into confusion, but, whatever the cause, Molotov showed himself more responsive than I could have believed possible. Mr. Sam Sary, the chief Cambodian delegate, had his way. He was given an agreeable program on dates and timetable and was reassured about his country's commitments under the Geneva accords.

This robust protagonist was soon to fall out with Norodom Sihanouk, his King, who was to step down from his throne to become Prime Minister. In this new role he pursued a course so devious as to perplex and sometimes to exasperate his foreign well-wishers. Through these twists and turns, more leftward than rightward, Sihanouk preserved two articles of faith intact. First, his country was to be truly neutral like Sweden or Switzerland, never to form part of a so-called neutralist bloc like Indonesia or Egypt; secondly, a neutrality guaranteed by the Geneva powers of 1954 held, in his conviction, the most hopeful promise for his people and his neighbors. It is still the best hope for peace, for all nations, that his faith should be fulfilled.

CHAPTER VI

TWELVE POINTS

VI

THE FOLLOWING are the conclusions which can be drawn
from my argument:

1. That the Geneva Agreements of 1954 can most use-
   fully serve as the framework for the ceasefire negotiations and for the terms of any guaranteed settlement.
2. That the membership of the Geneva Conference
   should be retained, i.e., the United States, the U.S.S.R.,
   China, the United Kingdom, France, Laos, Cambodia,
   North and South Vietnam.
3. That the co-chairmen of the Conference, the U.S.S.R.
   and the United Kingdom, should continue to function,
   their responsibilities being defined.
4. That the present membership of the Supervisory Commission, India, Canada and Poland, should be continued. The powers of the Commission should be defined and extended. It should be its responsibility to
   report its findings at stated intervals and in any

emergency to the Conference, through the channel of the co-chairmen.

5. That any agreement should guarantee the territories and the neutrality of Laos and Cambodia, offering the same opportunity to South and North Vietnam.

6. That the guarantees should be endorsed by all the powers represented at the Conference.

7. That the guarantees to be offered to North and South Vietnam, Laos and Cambodia should be joint and several, on the Locarno model, the guarantors having the right in certain conditions to act without waiting for unanimity, should the terms of the agreement be violated.

8. That the guaranteed countries should be denied the purchase of arms from any guarantor power, this prohibition being supervised by the Commission.

9. That a sufficient period must be allowed to elapse after the ceasefire for the economy and security of South and North Vietnam to be established. A short-term neutralization scheme has no possibility of success. A period of ten to fifteen years should be allowed before South and North Vietnam are called upon to decide their mutual relationship. This term could be reduced by agreement between the two parties, the co-chairmen and the Commission.

10. That the scheme for the use of the waters of the

Mekong River, now being prepared by the United Nations, should be prosecuted with the utmost despatch.

11. That the Geneva Prisoners of War Convention should be strictly observed.

12. That military plans and movements should be dovetailed into the political program laid down by the Conference, whose first duty should be to give instructions for determining a ceasefire.

While the above proposals cannot bring an immediate solution to the political problems of Indochina, nor one wholly satisfactory to any of the contending parties, they would make it possible for these territories, after twenty years of war, to cease to be a point of danger and to earn a better life in peace.

NOTES

1. *New York Times,* July 22, 1954. See the Appendix for the text of the final declaration of the Geneva Conference and the text of the unilateral declaration by the United States.
2. *New York Times,* May 7, 1954.
3. *New York Times,* Oct. 25, 1954.
4. Arthur M. Schlesinger, Jr., *A Thousand Days,* Boston: (Houghton Mifflin Co., 1965), p. 536.
5. *Ibid.,* p. 537.
6. *Documents relating to British Involvement in the Indo-China Conflict,* Cmnd. No. 2834, London: (Her Majesty's Stationery Office, 1965), p. 263.
7. *Idem.*
8. Paul Ely, *L'Indochine dans la Tourmente,* Paris: (Plon, 1964), p. 258.

APPENDIX

The Final Declaration of the Geneva Conference
21 July 1954

The Unilateral U.S. Declaration

The Final Declaration of the Geneva Conference
21 July 1954

This document, signed by the representatives of France, Great Britain, the Soviet Union, the People's Republic of China, the three Associated States, and the Vietminh Government, was worded as follows:

(1) The conference takes note of the agreements ending hostilities in Cambodia, Laos, and Vietnam, and organizing international control and supervision of the execution of the provisions of these agreements.

(2) The conference expressed satisfaction at the ending of hostilities in Cambodia, Laos, and Vietnam. It expresses its conviction that the execution of the provisions set out in the present declaration and in the agreements on the cessation of hostilities will permit Cambodia, Laos, and Vietnam henceforth to play their part, in full independence and sovereignty, in the peaceful community of nations.

(3) The conference takes note of the declarations made by the Governments of Cambodia and Laos of their

[69]

intention to adopt measures permitting all citizens to take their place in the national community, in particular by participating in the next general elections, which, in conformity with the Constitution of each of these countries, shall take place in 1955 by secret ballot and in conditions of respect for fundamental freedoms.

(4) The conference takes note of the clauses in the agreement on the cessation of hostilities in Vietnam prohibiting the introduction into Vietnam of foreign troops and military personnel, as well as of all kinds of arms and munitions. It also takes note of the declarations made by the Governments of Cambodia and Laos of their resolution not to request foreign aid, whether in war material, personnel, or instructors, except for the purpose of the effective defence of their territory and, in the case of Laos, to the extent defined by the agreements on the cessation of hostilities in Laos.

(5) The conference takes note of the clauses in the agreement on the cessation of hostilities in Vietnam to the effect that no military base at the disposition of a foreign State may be established in the regrouping zones of the two parties, the latter having the obligation to see that the zones allotted to them shall not constitute part of any military alliance and shall not

be utilized for the resumption of hostilities or in the service of an aggressive policy. The conference also takes note of the declarations of the Governments of Cambodia and Laos to the effect that they will not join in any agreement with other States if this agreement includes the obligation to participate in a military alliance not in conformity with the principles of the U.N. Charter or, in the case of Laos, with the principles of the agreement on the cessation of hostilities in Laos, or, so long as their security is not threatened, the obligation to establish bases on Cambodian or Laotian territory for the military forces of foreign Powers.

(6) The conference recognizes that the essential purpose of the agreement relating to Vietnam is to settle military questions with a view to ending hostilities, and that the military demarcation line should not in any way be interpreted as constituting a political or territorial boundary. It expresses its conviction that the execution of the provisions set out in the present declaration and in the agreement on the cessation of hostilities creates the necessary basis for the achievement in the near future of a political settlement in Vietnam.

(7) The conference declares that, so far as Vietnam is concerned, the settlement of political problems, ef-

fected on the basis of respect for the principles of independence, unity, and territorial integrity, shall permit the Vietnamese people to enjoy the fundamental freedoms, guaranteed by democratic institutions, established as a result of free general elections by secret ballot. To ensure that sufficient progress in the restoration of peace has been made, and that all the necessary conditions obtain for free expression of the national will, general elections shall be held in July, 1956, under the supervision of an International Commission composed of representatives of the member States of the International Supervisory Commission, referred to in the agreements on the cessation of hostilities. Consultations will be held on this subject between the competent representative authorities of the two zones from July, 1955, onwards.

(8) The provisions of the agreements on the cessation of hostilities intended to ensure the protection of individuals and of property must be most strictly applied and must, in particular, allow everyone in Vietnam to decide freely in which zone he wishes to live.

(9) The competent representative authorities of the northern and southern zones of Vietnam, as well as the authorities of Laos and Cambodia, must not permit any individual or collective reprisals against per-

sons who have collaborated in any way with one of the parties during the war, or against members of such a person's family.

(10) The conference takes note of the declaration of the French Government to the effect that it is ready to withdraw its troops from Cambodia, Laos, and Vietnam at the request of the Governments concerned and within a period which shall be fixed by agreement between the two parties, except in the cases where, by agreement between the two parties, a certain number of French troops shall remain at specified points and for a specified time.

(11) The conference takes note of the declaration of the French Government to the effect that, for the settlement of all problems connected with the re-establishment and consolidation of peace in Cambodia, Laos, and Vietnam, it will proceed from the principle of respect for the independence, sovereignty, unity, and territorial integrity of Cambodia, Laos, and Vietnam.

(12) In their relations with Cambodia, Laos, and Vietnam, each member of the Geneva Conference undertakes to respect the sovereignty, independence, unity, and territorial integrity of the above-mentioned States, and to refrain from any interference in their internal affairs.

(13) The members of the Conference agree to consult one

another on any questions which may be referred to them by the International Supervisory Commission in order to study such measures as may prove necessary to ensure that the agreements on the cessation of hostilities in Cambodia, Laos, and Vietnam are respected.

The Unilateral U.S. Declaration

The following unilateral declaration by the U.S. Government was issued by Mr. Bedell Smith:

The Government of the United States, being resolved to devote its efforts to the strengthening of peace in accordance with the principles and purposes of the United Nations;

Takes note of the agreements concluded at Geneva on July 20 and 21, 1954, between *(a)* the Franco-Laotian Command and the Command of the People's Army of Vietnam [i.e., the Vietminh military authorities]; *(b)* the Royal Cambodian Command and the People's Army of Vietnam; *(c)* the Franco-Vietnamese Command and the Command of the People's Army of Vietnam; and of paragraphs (1) to (12) inclusive of the declaration presented to the Geneva Conference on July 21, 1954;

Declares with regard to the aforesaid agreements and paragraphs that:

[75]

(1) It will refrain from the threat or the use of force to disturb them, in accordance with Article 2 (4) of the U.N. Charter dealing with the obligation of members to refrain in their international relations from the threat or use of force; and

(2) It would view any renewal of aggression in violation of the aforesaid agreements with grave concern and as seriously threatening international peace and security.

In connexion with the statement in the declaration concerning free elections in Vietnam, my Government wishes to make clear its position, which it has expressed in a declaration made in Washington on June 29, 1954 [by President Eisenhower and Sir Winston Churchill] as follows: "In the case of nations now divided against their will, we shall continue to seek to achieve unity through free elections, supervised by the U.N. to ensure that they are conducted fairly."

With respect to the statement made by the representative of the State of Vietnam, the United States reiterates its traditional position that peoples are entitled to determine their own future and that it will not join in an arrangement which would hinder this. Nothing in this declaration is intended to, or does, indicate any departure from this traditional position.

Appendix

We share the hope that the agreements will permit Cambodia, Laos and Vietnam to play their part, in full independence and sovereignty, in the peaceful community of nations, and will enable the peoples of that area to determine their own future.